Rock Climbing Technique

Rock Climbing Technique

The Practical Guide to Movement Mastery

John Kettle

Copyright © 2018 John Kettle

The moral right of the author has been asserted.

All rights reserved.
No part of this publication may be reproduced, stored in a retrieval system, or transmitted, in any form or by any means, without the prior permission in writing of the publisher, nor be otherwise circulated in any form of binding or cover other than that in which it is published and without a similar condition including this condition being imposed on the subsequent purchaser.

Published by John Kettle

Print ISBN 978-1-9996544-0-5
EPUB ISBN 978-1-9996544-1-2

Typesetting services by bookow.com

For Sue and Emily

Acknowledgments

A debt of gratitude is owed to many people who supported and encouraged me in this project: My editor Kirsten Donovan, videographer Jan Bella, Paul Smith, Steve Passiouras and my proof readers and testers Esther Foster, Ben Francis, Al Halewood, Zoltan Monostori, Rob Mulligan, Chris Pretty, Rebecca Ranstead, Taylor Reed.

A big thank you to the Lakeland Climbing Centre for supporting my growing independent business in their midst. Thank you also to all the climbers, instructors, guides and coaches I've had the privilege of spending time with, coaching and learning from over the last twenty-two years.

Numerous authors and researchers have informed and inspired my learning, and given me the foundation of knowledge upon which to develop my own ideas.

Last, but not least, to my amazing wife Sue and wonderful daughter Emily for their endless patience and loving support.

This book is intended as an adventure and an exploration of climbing movement. Like any adventure worth having, it will not be an easy journey but with a commitment to work hard on your climbing technique, great gains in personal performance and fulfilment can be had.

Personal responsibility for safety

Climbing is an activity with a danger of personal injury or death. This book provides no safety advice for climbers. Participants in these activities should be aware of and accept these risks and be personally responsible for their own actions.

Contents

Introduction		1
Potential Barriers to Improving Your Technique		4
1 Feet		**7**
Hello Feet		8
Exercise 1: Seriously Silent Ninja Feet		10
Exercise 2: Two Feet On		11
Exercise 3: Platform Builder		13
Exercise 4: Straight Arm, Bendy Body		14
Twisting		15
Exercise 5: Hip and Hand		16
Exercise 6: The Big Three		17
Dynamic Foot Movement		18
Exercise 7: The Leg Spring		19
Flagging		21
Exercise 8: The Can-Can		22
Exercise 9: The Button		25
Exercise 10: Button & Can-Can		27
Exercise 11: Can-Can & Hip and Hand		28
Exercise 12: The Inside-Outside Can-Can		29
The Final Exam – Exercises 13 and 14		30
Geeks' Corner		33

2	**Fingers**	**35**
	Hello Fingers	35
	Drag Grip Familiarity	40
	Exercise 15: The Sloth	41
	Hand Accuracy	42
	Exercise 16: Finger Ninja	43
	Finger Strength	44
	Geeks' Corner	45
3	**Core**	**47**
	Hello Core	48
	Exercise 17: The Butt Squeeze	51
	Exercise 18: Hip and Hand Progression	53
	Momentous Moves – The Four Springs	55
	Exercise 19: The Pendulum	57
	Exercise 20: The Corkscrew	60
	Exercise 21: Knee-Throw Variation	62
	Exercise 22: The Leg Thrust	64
	Exercise 23: One-Hand Variation	66
	Exercise 24: The Core Pop	68
	Exercise 25: Shoulder Pop Variation	70
	Exercise 26: Hip Pop Variation	72
	Exercise 27: Head Fling Variation	74
	Geeks' Corner	76
4	**Tension**	**79**
	Hello Muscles	80
	Exercise 28: The Tension Tester	81
	Hello Breathing	83
	Exercise 29: The Breath Sink	84
	Exercise 30: Sink to Zero Progression	85
	Exercise 31: Core Pressure	86
	Move Like It's Easy	87
	Exercise 32: Slackjaw	88
	Geeks' Corner	89

Contents

5	**Move Reading**	**91**
	Hello Memory: Move Recall	92
	Exercise 33: Plan, Climb, Review	93
	From Boulders to Routes	95
	Exercise 34: Chunking	96
	Exercise 35: Highlights	98
	Exercise 36: Speed Chunking	101
	Geeks' Corner	102
6	**Strategy**	**105**
	Focusing Your Play	105
	Quality Standards:	
	An Alternative Measure of Success	108
	Focusing on the Process	111
	Exercise 37: Micro Goals	112
	Geeks' Corner	113
7	**Quick Wins**	**117**
	Traditional Climbing	117
	Sport Climbing and Bouldering	118
Conclusion		**121**
Glossary		**123**

Introduction

Improving climbing technique can mean many things. Increasing efficiency is one aspect which allows you to climb harder at any given fitness level. Effortless, fluid movement is another. The accompanying feelings of mastery can open the door to a deeply rewarding experience on rock. It can also mean finding flow, experiencing climbing as a dance or a way to celebrate movement and express physical creativity.

Investing in your climbing skills is always worthwhile and doesn't demand a consistent time commitment. If you have limited opportunities to climb regularly, physical training can feel like pouring water into a leaky barrel: you must keep pouring all the time just to maintain a level. To increase the level you must pour faster and faster and if you stop, the level steadily decreases.

Skills development is far less dependent on consistent input. You can practise whenever you can - sometimes more, sometimes less, depending on circumstances. If you take a break for a few months, those skills are still embedded and you can continue to develop them further.

If you have an enforced layoff from fitness training - perhaps due to injury – skill development is a great way to maintain motivation and keep improving, while paving the way for excellent performance when you return to form. While I am enjoying the richness of life outside climbing, my own 'maintenance schedule' of up-skilling typically sees me climbing around twice a month. This is enough for me to continue gently consolidating my skill level, in anticipation of periods when I can devote more time to getting 'climbing fit'.

How to use this Book

This book contains five chapters, each focused on a specific area of the body or a specific climbing technique, including a range of practical exercises to introduce and develop skills which can be done at any climbing wall. Chapter Six explores how to apply it all to your climbing and Chapter Seven contains the 'quick fixes' for those really short of time.

Many of the practical exercises are accompanied by a demonstration video, in addition to the written description and illustrations. If you have access to a tablet or smart phone, watching these videos will ensure you learn quickly and easily. There are links to the videos in the e-book version of this publication and they are freely accessible online. From the paper version of this book, you can reach them by scanning the QR code on your mobile device, typing the web address into your browser or by visiting youtube.com and searching for my channel by name.

I have set aside space at the end of each chapter for you to record your personal reflections and experiences and make notes for future reference. Take the book and videos with you when you go climbing, note down your answers to the questions or, better still, involve your climbing partners. Their feedback and observations will highlight things you may otherwise miss. Many of the exercises will challenge your awareness of your body, and be difficult to complete. Take careful note of which are hardest for you and revisit them regularly in your climbing. Keeping notes will allow you to track progress and organise your practice to ensure you always target your weakest areas.

If you are a coach, or want to know more on a topic, every chapter includes a *'Geeks' Corner'* just for you. It includes recommended reading, background theories and introductions to additional topics to take you further down the rabbit hole.

Technique and Injury

How you move has a huge influence on your chances of getting injured, from posture and breathing through to hold preference and right- or left-side dominance. I coach people of all ages with chronic elbow, shoulder and finger problems. Often their injuries can be reduced or allowed to fully recover through simple adjustments in their movement.

Compare the size of your quadriceps (quads) to your forearms – can you tell which have evolved to carry your bodyweight? The significant risk that accompanies the training of smaller muscles, such as those in the arms, is that overstepping their capability leads to injury. Injuries are extremely common in climbers, more so since the rise in popularity of indoor walls and bouldering centres. Training technique doesn't carry the same level of risk as physical training does. Over-doing it is only likely to lead to zen-like levels of mastery.

Beyond improving individual techniques, it's about enlarging the number of movements in your repertoire - think of it as increasing *movement literacy*. Poor movement literacy correlates to increased injury risk, and performance limitations.

Choosing role models

We all recognise that grade is an unreliable measure of technical skill, simply because you can compensate for poor technique with other strengths, even at a world class level.

When you are looking for role-models of excellent technique, seek out the *optimal performer* - a climber who is improbably weak for their grade, not a musclebound powerhouse or *high level compensator*. Then you will get to see someone who employs training, tactics and movement to the highest degree.

Potential Barriers to Improving Your Technique

Beliefs and Ego

Climbing skill is something acquired with practice, not a trait you were born with, or without. Two years ago I achieved what would typically be called a lifetime goal, pulling over the top of my first 8A/V11 boulder problem. However, it was so far beyond what I believed was achievable in my lifetime that had you predicted it five years ago, when I had a young family and after double shoulder surgery, I'd have been extremely dubious. Sixteen years ago, when I'd been climbing for five years and when 6C/V4 seemed utterly desperate, I would have flatly refused to believe it possible. My point is that lifetime goals from my physical 'prime' when I was single and time-rich now look pathetic compared to what I can achieve under

Introduction

more constrained circumstances. How much further I can go remains a compelling mystery since I've repeatedly underestimated my potential in the past. The future really is unwritten - could you shatter your current expectations?

Learning is about change, which is fundamentally uncomfortable for our fragile egos.

Looking daft, doing things differently and failing a lot are all great reasons to avoid the rocky road to mastery. Sticking to the path of least resistance and mediocrity will always feel more comfortable.

If you are prepared to battle mentally on climbs you usually cruise then the exercises in this book will lead to a flowing and effortless climbing experience.

Awareness: The Unconscious Barrier

> 'These three things are hard: steel, diamond and to know thyself'
>
> - Benjamin Franklin,
> one of The Founding Fathers of the United States

When a climber fails on a route they instinctively ask themselves what is limiting their climbing ability. Pain, or that searing pump in your forearms, is the loudest feedback we receive from our bodies. The climber concludes that if their forearms hadn't exploded by the seventh bolt, they would have been more successful. So begins the pursuit of physical strength and fitness as a route to improvement.

What may have been overlooked is other more subtle feedback that relies on higher levels of bodily awareness. How a climber thinks, moves and breathes influences their results, sometimes much more than fitness and strength.

The reason most people don't work hard on developing good technique is a lack of awareness that there is scope for improvement.

Some of My Mistakes

I was oblivious to climbing technique for fifteen years - I was strong, reasonably flexible and never once considered backing off when things got tricky. This guns-blazing approach yielded a decade of steady improvements, gripping experiences and some large trad falls. It also brought seven years of tennis and golfer's elbow, countless finger tweaks and two show-stopping shoulder injuries by the age of twenty-eight. By this point my shoulders allowed me to climb gently only once a week, so fitness gains were out of the question. I'd had some fantastic times climbing, met my wife and earned a living teaching and guiding but I seriously considered ditching it at this point because of the pain and frustration. Progress, which had been my main motivator, looked impossible. After a year of unsuccessful shoulder rehab I started to work on technique out of desperation and was enlightened. My technique was terrible, my posture was pitiful and my tactics atrocious! The veil of awareness was lifted. Three years later, both shoulders were surgically repaired and I had a family, a mortgage and many new time constraints. Despite this, over the last decade I have steadily improved at trad and sport climbing and bouldering, both in terms of performance and enjoyment.

Awareness was my barrier, could it be yours?

Chapter 1

Feet

'*Climbing is a rear wheel drive sport*'

– *British rock climber Johnny Dawes*

Good footwork underpins high-quality movement in every excellent climber. While most climbers recognise that footwork is important, many fail to explore it beyond a basic level. Poor habits build and are steadily reinforced through decades of climbing practice.

As half of our contact points with the rock, feet play a similar role to hands for climbers but, unlike our hands, they're attached to limbs that can easily support our bodyweight for long periods of time. How efficiently our legs take our weight often decides the fate of our forearms a dozen moves into a climb. Bear your weight well, in best balance, and you will still be fresh for the hardest crux moves. Miss opportunities to improve balance via foot positioning and you will fatigue far faster. This means you are much more dependent on forearm fitness. Our hands are in easy sight, extremely sensitive and well-practiced at small complex movements, for example typing. Contrast this with our feet which are out of sight and mind, less sensitive and far less co-ordinated for fine movements. Expecting them to just 'step up' and perform like our hands when climbing is unrealistic unless we commit to giving them the loving attention and training they deserve:

Hello Feet

Let's begin by tuning in to our most distant points of contact and see what they are really getting up to. For this exercise pick a wall with lots of large holds, either vertical or a slab, which presents no difficulty and causes no anxiety for you to climb. This will probably mean climbing on a top rope, auto belay or low-level traverse so all your attention is focused on observing your feet. Choose just one question per ascent and climb repeatedly until you can confidently answer the following:

- How many foot placements do I use on this wall?

- How many times do both feet point left?

- How many times do both feet point right?

- How many times do both feet point at the wall (toe on)?

- How many times do both feet point away from my body (inside edges)?

At this point you can perhaps answer these two questions without climbing again:

- Which is my preferred stance – left pointing, right pointing, toe on or inside edges?

Feet

- What effect do these stances have on my hip position?

The next three questions will very likely require further climbing before you can answer them:

- How many times do I tap, adjust or bounce a foot more than half a millimetre after placing it on a hold during one ascent?

- How many times do I make contact with the wall first and need to slide my foot down more than half a millimetre to the hold?

- Which foot is more accurate, left or right?

If you can answer all these questions with certainty, well done - have a lie down. There are many possibilities for you to now explore with your footwork. The suggestions below are just a few of those.

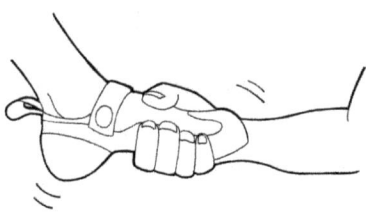

Rock Climbing Technique

Exercise 1: Seriously Silent Ninja Feet

This is the logical step once you have answered the final three questions, or are trying to avoid assassination whilst climbing:

Ascend an easy wall on rainbow holds, making as few foot taps or unnecessary adjustments as possible and paying particular attention to your least accurate foot.

Don't count deliberate pivoting on the feet, just unplanned movements, and strive for excellence, not perfection.

Exercise 2: Two Feet On

This exercise can prove challenging for fans of flagging, where you stand on one leg with the other extended to the side.

Climb on an easy wall, using all holds and follow this rule:

Both feet must remain on holds for the duration of every hand move.

Essentially this prevents three things: flagging, finishing hand moves with one foot off and choosing one-footed static positions when clipping and chalking. If you find this challenging it suggests that habitual flagging may be part of your current routine. You will benefit from practising this drill until it takes no more mental effort than normal climbing.

When standing on the floor, do you balance on one foot as a matter of course? Are you actually a Flamingo? If not, best balance means finding at least two contact points to support your weight against gravity. When climbing, this usually means having both feet on holds, but it could be anything you can lean on to relieve strain on the forearms and transfer the effort onto bigger muscle groups. One example of this is when chimney climbing.

There are two reasons why many climbers choose to stand on one leg more than is absolutely necessary:

youtu.be/aPmPFPk_2kc

Rock Climbing Technique

Our Lazy Brain: It's less mental effort to pick one foothold to move from, rather than two, and we have lazy brains. We make a little more *physical* effort to experience a bit less *mental* effort. This can be overcome with practice. Once it is no extra mental effort to pick two footholds for every hand move, this is what the body will opt for as it is more efficient physically. Making physically efficient movement mentally effortless is the holy grail of mastering climbing technique!

Anxiety-Led Decision Making: When we first begin climbing, we are often anxious. We want to hold big holds as often as possible, so our attention is drawn upwards in search of the next jug. We stretch for these, not noticing if we have taken a foot off a hold in the process and we are now out of balance. We only sort out our feet after latching the hold. This can develop into a habitual pattern of hand-led climbing that goes 'grab handhold, sort out balance' over and over.

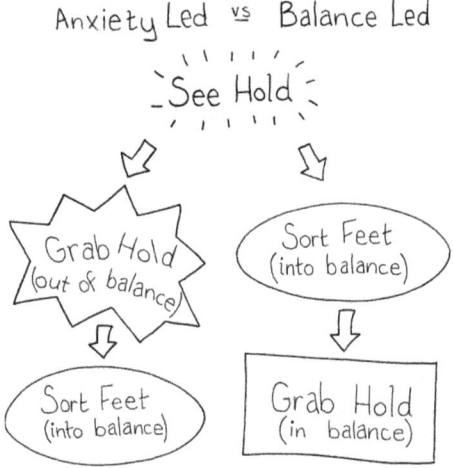

If getting into balance changed from an afterthought to the number one priority, we would set up our feet perfectly every time in order to make each hand move as easy as possible.

Exercise 3: Platform Builder

Imagine a plank running between the soles of your feet. Your hips need to stay vertically above this platform in order for you to be in a stable position. It's okay for the platform to slope left or right, as long as your hips remain vertically above it.

> Repeat the **Two Feet On** exercise but this time construct the imaginary platform with your feet for every hand move, ensuring it isn't changed unless both hands are on holds.

This exercise encourages a shift towards balance-led decision making, an altogether different way of thinking your way up a climb for many.

youtu.be/wFFTpqGGzMg

Exercise 4: Straight Arm, Bendy Body

Performing this exercise well demands creative use of your torso and legs, both of which depend on your footwork choices.

> For the duration of every hand move, the other arm which is holding on must remain straight. Begin on easy vertical to lightly overhanging terrain with many big holds.

Reducing mobility in the upper body is guaranteed to reveal whether a climber positions themselves using their arms, body or feet. Some climbers pull themselves into balance with their arms. Others rearrange their feet to balance and can keep the arm straight. Even when footholds are limited, bending the legs and twisting the trunk can often result in balance without pulling on the arms. Do you find it easier to keep the left or the right arm straight?

Getting comfortable with this exercise confirms you can use footwork and body positioning to minimise arm involvement. This means you will have more strength left for the crux and happier elbows in the long term, with a reduced risk of injury. If you are finding it strenuous on easy terrain, rearrange your feet to support your weight better as per the Platform Builder exercise and check you are not flagging unnecessarily.

youtu.be/yG2fvVrhc_c

Twisting

Twisting of hips and torso is a fundamental movement skill for climbing vertical and overhanging terrain. Many climbers start their apprenticeship on gently angled walls and slabs. While this usually means more early successes, it can also mean that slab techniques such as front-on climbing get much more development because steeper faces are initially avoided.

Under the stress of a steep and strenuous climb, this can lead to the climber applying what they know best, rather than adapting their style to suit the terrain. Being equally comfortable side-on as front-on, and being able to pivot from one side to the other, are key to moving with great efficiency on steep walls, overhangs and boulders.

Rock Climbing Technique

Exercise 5: Hip and Hand

This is a classic method to familiarise yourself with efficient twisting techniques and the cunning footwork they require.

For the duration of every hand move, the same hip must be against the wall as the moving hand.

Perform this on vertical or gently overhanging walls with many big holds.

Several skills are tested by this exercise including the climber's familiarity with side-on movement and the ability to position their body to allow efficient twisting. When you are confident performing this drill, it will be easier to spot opportunities to turn side on, pivot between positions and clip or chalk with the appropriate - inside - arm when side-on. If you have a preferred side to face, you will find it is tempting not to pivot back to the other side for each hand move. Becoming comfortable at turning will ensure that you don't just stick to your favoured side when stressed on hard routes, missing easier sequences in the process. If you find it tiring on easy terrain, check whether you're flagging a lot and whether your 'platform building' is supporting your weight.

youtu.be/GS_ByeGPQcY

Exercise 6: The Big Three

Combine **Hip and Hand** with **Two Feet On** and **Straight Arm, Bendy Body** to provide a stern test of creative and efficient footwork: For the duration of every hand move the same hip must be against the wall as the moving hand, both feet must remain on holds and the other arm which is holding on must remain straight.

Try this too early on and your brain will implode. Get the three exercises polished up individually, adding in one more at a time and always monitoring the effect it has on the rest of your movement.

youtu.be/7PH6HJ9q4jk

Dynamic Foot Movement

Minimising time spent standing on one leg is a good idea but inevitably this occurs for a few seconds each time we move a foot. If we are in a stable position with our weight fully over the other leg this may not tax our arms. This is frequently not possible however, and during these times the arms must work momentarily harder while we establish a new foothold. It often requires moving out of balance and one way we can buy this time is with physical effort, through tightening the upper body. Alternatively, if we are well-practiced, we can buy this time by creating momentum with the legs and thus save precious arm strength for the crux moves.

Like any dynamic climbing movement, this requires a high degree of skill and accuracy. It is mentally tougher to execute than when you have all the time your arms can endure to leisurely move your foot. Purposeful practice is therefore paramount to success, but in risky situations where high levels of precision are required, static movement is safer, albeit more tiring.

Exercise 7: The Leg Spring

All of the force for dynamic foot-moves should come from the lowest leg – the one you are about to move. Dropping down before springing up feels strange to most climbers, despite it being the way we perform a standing jump when on the floor. Check nobody you want to impress is watching and try these on a top rope on an easy angled slab with lots of holds:

> Get into a 'ready to rock-over' position with one foot higher than the other and both hands around eye height. Drop your weight down onto the lower leg, flexing the knee, then spring up to place the foot on a new hold, higher than the other foot. Rearrange both hands to eye height again and repeat the foot spring with the other leg. Continue crouching and springing up the slab, only moving your hands between foot moves.

Once you are familiar with this pattern of movement, repeat the climb, focusing on holding and pulling as little as possible with the hands. Deliberately exaggerate the flexing of the lower knee and feel when the upper leg and arms take over to finish the move. Ideally, this should be as late as possible. Try really tall explosive rockovers, wide sideways moves and subtle small steps. Check it's the powerful quad muscles you are using to spring off, rather than the calf muscles in a 'heel bob'.

youtu.be/rjdWKkGP00g

Rock Climbing Technique

Set up.. ..Drop down.. ..Spring up

You may notice that it is easier to spring from the leg you want to move when there is more weight on it. Wide stance moves and high rockovers are where it can have the greatest impact, removing the need for strenuous pulling. Try it ascending a corner or bridging up a chimney.

Not every foot move ends on another hold, so to put the leg spring into context we need to be comfortable using it for three different means:

1. **Spring to another foothold:** The first choice of the discerning rock maestro. Getting two feet on means optimal balance, core engagement and minimal arm effort.

2. **Spring to one-legged balance:** This is the second best, often found on slabs and in situations where very precise foot placement is required before the next spring is initiated.

3. **Spring to a handhold:** This is last on the list and requires a large amount of core tension to execute well. The feet need to be repositioned to support the body as soon as possible after the hold is

caught. Novice climbers, or those that are hand-oriented, often lunge to hand holds and then sort their feet out as an afterthought. It means spending much more time in poor balance.

Find an easy-graded slab, groove or corner and ascend it in a series of deliberate foot springs. Observe how many times you make each of the three springs described above. Can you maximise the number of springs to another foothold?

One of the greatest benefits of this exercise is the downward foot-focus it encourages. For climbers whose handhold obsession keeps them looking upwards, time devoted to pressing and springing feet up a climb can be a liberating experience. Handholds come within easy reach if foot positioning is correct. Balance becomes a focus of movement while over-gripping and rushed, noisy feet become a distant memory.

Flagging

Using one leg to 'flag' is key to achieving best balance when you've paused on one foot. Some styles of flagging come intuitively to most, while others have to be purposefully practised if they are to be mastered. A word of caution before you set to work perfecting your flagging skills: The most common issue I observe is over-use.

Indoor climbing with its widely-spaced footholds has led many people to habitually use one foot rather than both. It is less mental effort to choose one foothold to move from rather than two, and as such is a shortcut to finding the sensation of effortless flowing movement. Unfortunately, it is also harder work standing on and moving from one leg rather than two. Consider excessive flagging a cognitive trap that sneakily robs you of forearm endurance one move at a time. If this sounds familiar, revisit **Exercise 2** to be sure you are not a compulsive flagger here to feed your shameful habit.

Rock Climbing Technique

Exercise 8: The Can-Can

For the duration of every hand move, only one foot can be on a hold.

Climbers may meet the constraints of the exercise in a variety of ways. First, there are three different kinds of flag, or you can dangle the leg vertically or hover it above a foothold. If you dangle or hover, it suggests lack of familiarity with flagging and an out-of-balance choice with the other foot. Notice where the supporting foot goes relative to your pelvis - is it offset to the side or directly beneath?

Continue to observe with curiosity what your feet get up to during further trials and answer these four questions:

youtu.be/suunPFxFuoo

1. Does it feel easiest when I'm facing left, right or front-on?
2. How many inside flags did I use?
3. How many outside flags did I use?
4. How many same-side flags did I use?

From these answers you will now know which types of flag you prefer - if any - and which types you neglect. At this point you have a choice:

- Run some quality assurance checks on your existing flagging – try Exercise 9: The Button

- Redress the balance by dusting down your least-used flags with Exercise 12: Inside-Outside Variation

- Treat yourself to a new chalk bag and try to forget all about it

Passive Versus Active Flagging

The flagging leg assists your balance by acting as a counterweight. It helps keep your centre of mass over your supporting foot when your body is offset to one side.

If the flagging leg isn't touching the wall, or is only lightly in contact, then it can only assist with balance and is regarded as a *passive flag*. Alternatively you can 'toe-in' hard to the wall with the flagging foot, as if pressing a button on the wall, taking weight from your shoulders to your core.

With this *active flag*, the toe can now be used to push off the wall for hand moves, meaning you can initiate movement with both legs, even when flagging.

Rock Climbing Technique

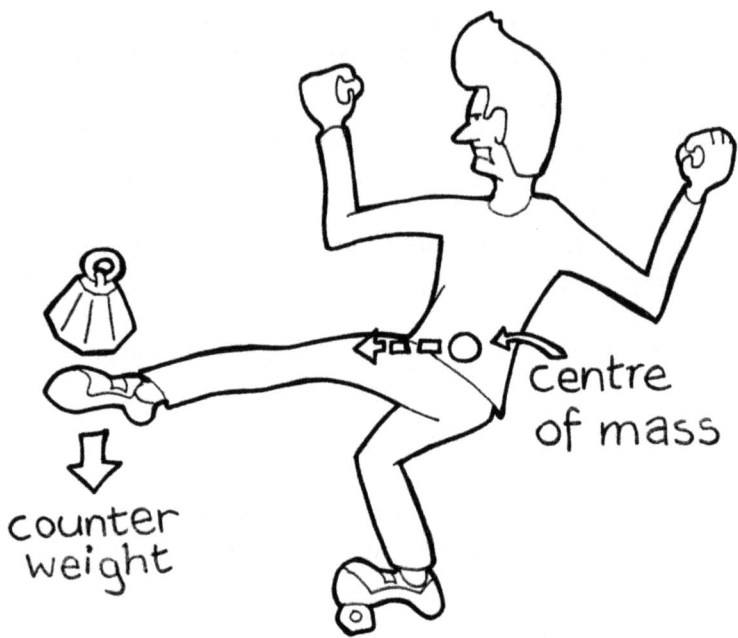

Exercise 9: The Button

Choose a same-side flagging position on the wall, flagging with your left foot and with your right hip in to the wall.

> Push your left big toe hard into the wall, as if you are pushing a button on the wall, and notice the extra tension it creates in your hips and glutes. Try moving the right hand from this position.

Compare shoulder and core tension between doing this with a passive left leg (held out in a flag) and an active left leg (pressing 'the button'). Progress to some further variations when you feel ready:

> Go Large: Now find a crouched passive flagging position and make a huge move with the right hand, finishing on straightened legs. Notice how the left leg either pivots outwards or drags up the wall as you extend through the move.
>
> Next, place 'the button' in a position that allows you to keep the left toe pressing it all the way through the hand move – just where you would ideally have a foothold. This will mean beginning a big move with a bent flagging leg.

youtu.be/DW6x42_yEu4

Rock Climbing Technique

Practicing on both sides, experiment with button placement using chalk dots and compare how different positions feel:

1. Can you press hard all the way through the move?
2. Is the leg bunched at the start, or dragging a little at the end of the move?
3. What happens when you place the button further up or down?
4. What happens when you place the button further left or right?

You will notice that the best button position depends on where the handhold is that you are aiming for. Big upward moves require a higher button and sideways moves need a button closer to the supporting leg.

If you have access to a symmetrical training board, compare your flagging skills on both sides. Finally, try applying the button technique to some inside and outside flags.

Does it help more for moving or holding positions?

Exercise 10: Button & Can-Can

Once you have identified how the different flagging techniques feel, try these more complex variations:

Apply **The Button** to every flag move during the **Can-Can** exercise: For the duration of every hand move, only one foot can be on a hold.

---

youtu.be/uros0WMF6fg

Rock Climbing Technique

Exercise 11: Can-Can & Hip and Hand

Continue to observe what your legs get up to and revisit the four questions in the **Can-Can**, while trying to:

Combine the Can-Can with Hip and Hand exercise: For the duration of every hand move the same hip must be against the wall as the moving hand, and only one foot can be on a hold.

---

youtu.be/nlGgMEXMkwE

Exercise 12: The Inside-Outside Can-Can

> For the duration of every hand move, the same hip must be against the wall as the moving hand and the same foot as the moving hand must be flagging. For example, the left hand moves with a left foot flag.

This will produce a mix of inside and outside flags but no same-side flags. If you wish to focus on just one flag type, work out which foot placements suit it best - for example high or low - and do repeat ascents using just that flag type.

Becoming confident with inside and outside flagging is key to reducing foot swapping. If you find yourself swapping feet to perform a same-side flag and then swapping back again to continue climbing, you missed an opportunity to perform an inside/outside flag and foot swapped twice instead. Foot swaps are hard on the arms and best minimised. This is a very common movement inefficiency when pausing to clip the rope or place trad gear.

youtu.be/Hx6JGCTDL-8

Rock Climbing Technique

The Final Exam – Exercises 13 and 14

Combine Straight Arm, Bendy Body with both Hip and Hand and Can-Can: For the duration of every hand move the same hip must be against the wall as the moving hand, only one foot can be on a hold, and the other arm which is holding on must remain straight.

---

youtu.be/rz6T0PmEXL8

Now try combining **Straight Arm, Bendy Body** with both **Hip and Hand** and the **Inside-Outside Can-Can**: For the duration of every hand move the same hip must be against the wall as the moving hand, the same foot as the moving hand must be flagging, and the other arm which is holding on must remain straight.

Expect DEFCON levels of brain fuzz if you haven't got the individual exercises wired.

youtu.be/hRLuNi0o0Sk

Rock Climbing Technique

Geeks' Corner

You may have noticed that bodily awareness is at the root of changing climbing movement. Somatics is a good place to start if you are curious about exploring this further. I recommend Todd Hargrove's *A Guide to Better Movement* as a good practical introduction as it builds on the more detailed work of somatic pioneers Thomas Hanna, Moshe Feldenkrais and Ida Rolf.

You may also have observed that many of the practical exercises in this chapter don't focus on what you should do, but rather draw attention to what you should not do. This has its foundation in 'Constraints-Led' skill acquisition theory. *Dynamics of Skill Acquisition* (Davids/Button/Bennett) covers both the theory and research in detail. *The Inner Game of Tennis* (Galway) also precedes the theory but encourages a similar approach to learning in a text that translates well to coaching of any sport.

Rock Climbing Technique

Chapter 2

Fingers

Our mind is highly sensitive to feedback from our hands and fingers, in contrast to our feet. Consequently, we tend to place them accurately and well from an early stage. Much has been written on finger anatomy, different ways to use handholds, grip types and the craft of jamming. This text focuses on developing excellent habits in general finger use, an overlooked skill which goes a long way to reducing finger-injury rates.

Hello Fingers

Let's begin by observing how we currently use our fingers. For this exercise pick a graded climb or traverse with a variety of holds, ideally with minimal jugs, that presents medium difficulty for you. A moderate bouldering circuit is also suitable for this process.

Check you are happy with the finger jargon, then climb repeatedly and record answers to the following questions:

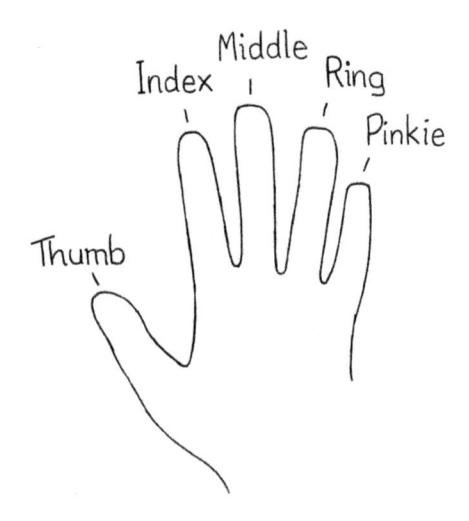

1. How many times do I half crimp with my:
   A) Pinkie finger B) Ring finger C) Middle finger D) Index finger
2. How many times do I crimp with my:
   A) Pinkie finger B) Ring finger C) Middle finger D) Index finger
3. How many times do I drag with my:
   A) Pinkie finger B) Ring finger C) Middle finger D) Index finger
4. How many times do I pinch with the thumb (regardless of hold shape)?

Well done if you've managed to answer all of them, you can stop frowning now. You may have noticed certain preferences in how you use your hands. As your fingers are often out of sight whilst climbing, these exercises require you to concentrate on the feel of your finger positions. If that's too hard, you can ask a friend to help observe.

What is your go-to finger configuration on flat holds and edges? Mine is with pinkie dragging and the other three half-crimping. Some other favourites are:

Fingers

- All four fingers crimping
- Pinkie and index dragging, middle two fingers half crimping
- Pinkie off and the others dragging

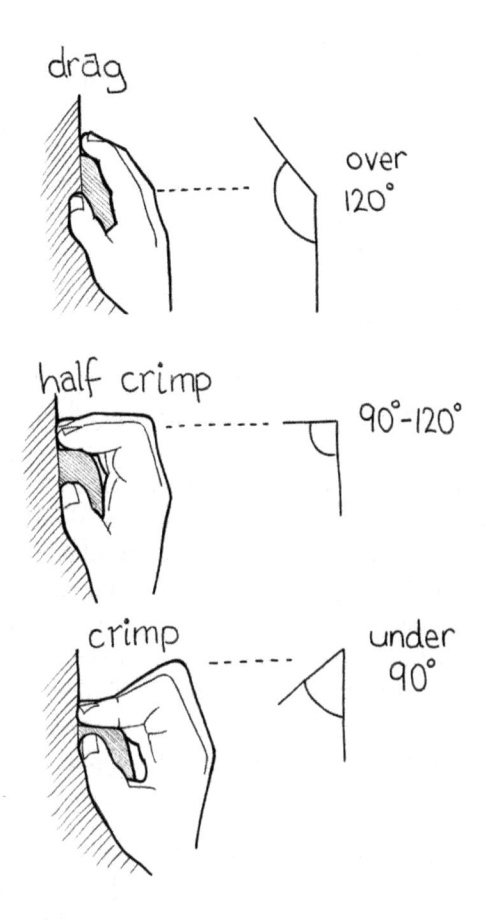

drag — over 120°

half crimp — 90°-120°

crimp — under 90°

Variation between climbers is partly to do with relative finger lengths - a fixed trait you needn't worry about - and habit, which is something you can definitely change.

Recognising which grip type you use most is invaluable in combating finger injuries. It allows you to modify finger habits and shape finger-strength training protocol, if you choose to follow one.

Our fingers are fundamentally not designed to bear our weight, so if we want to have a long and enjoyable climbing career it is key that we put thought into how to use them economically. Chapters One, Three, Four and Five are about doing everything possible with the rest of our bodies to reduce the load on our fingers. Finger, hand, wrist and forearm injuries occur in all grip positions. The most common injuries are pulley strain and tears and these can be caused by the excessive, habitual use of crimp grips. If we are not confident using the drag position with our fingers, we risk avoidable finger injuries.

Chronic Crimpers – why do I crimp everything?

Crimping is really popular with new climbers because it requires a lower skill level than dragging - witness the rampant sloper-phobia in any climbing wall. You can pull downward, outward and a little left and right on a crimp. Using the same hold in a drag means you can only pull downward, and it only takes a little outward pull to make it feel insecure. The trick to making slopers work for you lies in careful body positioning, whereas making a crimp more effective is often simply a matter of holding it tighter. Without the skill and familiarity that comes with purposeful sloper use, crimps can easily appear to be more useful holds.

Anxiety is another contributor to habitual crimping as fear encourages cautious movement, resulting in long slow reaches and deep 'lock-offs'. These require pulling outward on the locked-off hold as it moves below your shoulder, again encouraging crimping. There are plenty of times

Fingers

drag

effective pull angle

crimp

effective pull angle

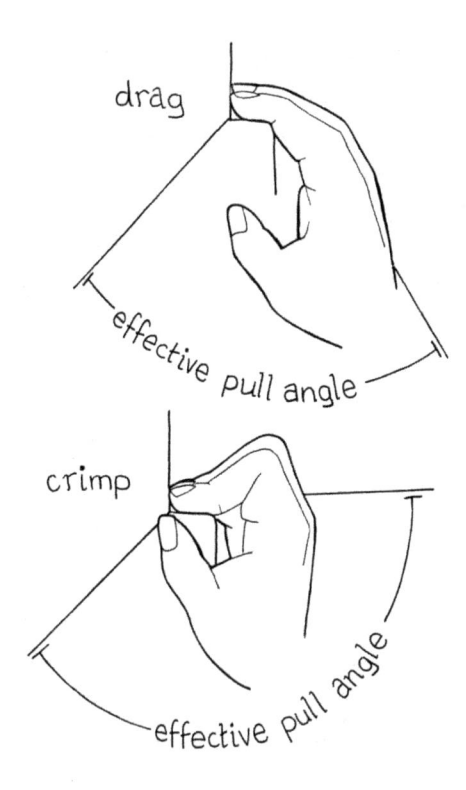

when cautious movement is a good idea. However, if it is your habitual style when three feet above a thick pad or safely by the sixth bolt, then you risk fast-tracking finger tweaks.

As a confident climber with years of experience, crimping may have embedded itself in your mind early on and still be a habit even when calm and focused. However, with skilful body positioning and utilisation of the core, drag (sloper) grips become far more versatile and attractive to use. With regular use comes the confidence and physical understanding that allows even further use, so crimping habits can be broken before the finger tendons themselves.

Rock Climbing Technique

Drag Grip Familiarity

Feeling relaxed and comfortable with an open-handed grip is a key skill for all climbers. Without this familiarity the mind will often shy away from opportunities to use this grip, preferring crimp-based grips instead. This drill isn't meant to represent the easiest way to climb but it fast-tracks drag grip mileage to redress grip habit imbalances. Choose an easy wall and if possible avoid leading on the first few ascents:

Exercise 15: The Sloth

> Climb the route using the three-finger drag grip position, where you use only the ring, middle and index fingers. Pinkies and thumbs are banned, half or full crimping is prohibited and wrapping your fingers all the way around jugs is illegal. Think three-toed sloth.

Notice how the sloth drill affects the rest of your body, and answer the following:

- Is there extra tension in your arms, neck or shoulders?

- Are you any more anxious than usual?

- Do you straighten your arms more or less?

- Are your hips closer to the wall or further out?

- Do you use undercling or sidepull holds any differently?

- What are the limitations of this grip type?

youtu.be/yG_3yhMvF08

Hand Accuracy

Deadpoints and other dynamic moves to small holds often constitute the crux of routes and boulder problems. Two options exist to increase the chance of successfully catching a small hold. The first is to slow down the movement so that you can be more accurate. This is safer if the fall holds a high risk but more strenuous for the other arm and relies heavily on crimping and locking off. Habitual long-term use of this style is hard on the shoulders, elbows and fingers.

The alternative is to improve hand accuracy so that at speed you consistently latch small or awkward holds that need to be caught a specific way. Habitual long-term use of this style makes you less dependent on lock-off strength and crimp power and therefore more efficient and generally awesome.

Exercise 16: Finger Ninja

> Traverse or climb an easy vertical wall, only moving both hands at the same time. Ensure both hands land simultaneously, increasing the pace as you become more confident.

By removing the option to look at each hold as your hand moves to it, this drill sharpens your ability to use proprioception - the awareness of where your body is in space - to guide your limbs. It is not always possible, or efficient, to keep the eyes on a hold during a dynamic hand move so good spatial awareness is essential.

Bouldering board variations:

- Compare left- and right-hand accuracy levels by creating single-move deadpoint challenges on a symmetrical systems board.

- Keeping the feet in one place, jump both hands up three pairs of holds and back down again. Offset left and right handholds at different heights for a greater challenge. If you cut loose, start again and pull harder with your feet - bad ninja.

youtu.be/XLYbQyPFcAE

Finger Strength

While physical training is outside the scope of this book, it is worth being aware that the strength of your fingers affects the range of movement available to you on small holds. If you are pulling at near maximal levels just to hold on, this muscle tension effectively fixes you in place. It reduces your options for twisting, setting up your feet well or initiating from the core with fluid hip movements. A long period of climbing with underperforming fingers can fix the rigid 'front-on snatching' style as a habit which is hard to correct even after the fingers have strengthened.

Geeks' Corner

Many existing books provide a good introduction to basic hand techniques. My favourite is *Advanced Rock Climbing* by Long/Luebben which also has a great section on jamming techniques. Dave MacLeod's *9 Out Of 10 Climbers Make the Same Mistakes* and his injury-focused follow-up *Make or Break*, both contain excellent information on hand strength training, the injury/technique interface and rehab protocol if it goes wrong. Eva Lopez has also conducted some great research and blogged extensively on finger-strength training alongside many other climbing training topics. Some interesting research data has been gathered over the last 15 years by the coaches at *Lattice Training*, linking hand strength to climbing grades. If you boulder V5 or redpoint 7b+/5.12 upwards, it may be worth exploring further.

The Finger Ninja exercise is an example of proprioceptive training. It can be applied with equal effectiveness, but greater difficulty, to foot movements and many other areas of movement.

Rock Climbing Technique

notes

Chapter 3

Core

CORE is a rather vague term. For the purpose of this chapter, it is the trunk muscles that stabilise your body in all climbing positions. At the four corners of the torso are highly mobile ball-and-socket joints. Your torso itself isn't immobile but needs to remain stable to safely manage the forces coming to it from your hands and feet whilst climbing. If your spine and pelvis are unstable, some of the smaller muscles of the mobiliser joints (hips and shoulders) or the peripheral limbs (knees and elbows) will need to pick up the burden and work extra hard. This leads to faster forearm fatigue in the short term and accelerated wear to the knees, shoulders, elbows and wrists in the long term. When watching a climber use minimal core muscles to stabilise their body, I often see tense arms, neck, shoulders and calves. Between this upper and lower body tension is a jelly-like trunk.

Awareness of your core and how it operates is something that reaches far wider than just rock climbing technique. Explore it as part of postural awareness in everything you do, particularly the mundane everyday movements that become habit-setters for a lifetime. How we breathe, sit and stand has a huge impact on our long-term health. It is easy to assume that being fit and active must mean we move well but this is often not the case, as becomes evident in middle age when wear and tear catches up with our backs, necks and shoulders. Any movement-based activity taught well can raise awareness of posture and re-train it where necessary: Pilates, yoga, power lifting and martial arts all offer great scope for better understanding and use of the core.

Hello Core

Your centre of mass is the moveable point around which your whole body would theoretically rotate, pivot or balance. When standing normally it is about two inches below the navel, set deep in the centre of the body. If you raise your arms, as if climbing, your centre of mass shifts upward, closer to your belly button.

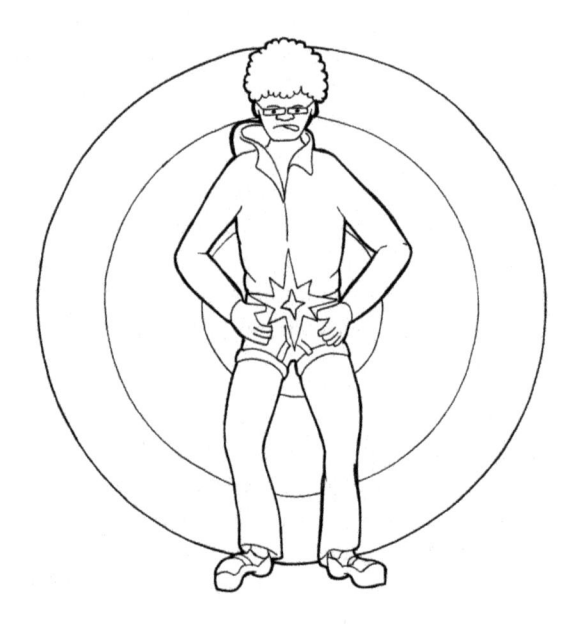

Finding Centre: The Supermagnet Laser

Developing a feel for where your centre of mass lies is fundamental to the next series of exercises. Let's begin with some relaxed observational climbs:

> Place an imaginary tracker in your centre of mass and observe the distance it is from the wall as you ascend.

Notice when it moves closer or further out and where it is if you pivot side on.

> Activate the 'supermagnet' on the tracker, which draws your centre of mass powerfully towards the (iron) wall that you are ascending. When climbing, try and keep the supermagnet as close to the wall as possible at all times.

Notice which muscles work harder and how it affects your movement. Is your core involved more?

> This time reverse the supermagnet so that your centre of mass is being repelled from the wall.

How does this compare in terms of physical and mental effort? For some climbers this is physically harder, but feels more familiar and mentally easier. This suggests a less efficient movement closer to their habitual style.

Rock Climbing Technique

> Turn off the magnet and activate the laser so it shines out of your centre of mass onto the wall. As you ascend, notice the squiggly line it traces up the wall.

Is this line mostly straight, curved, or with many sharp angles?

Can you repeat the climb tracing a more angular path, and a curvier one?

While lasers and supermagnets aren't essential tools, an ability to focus on your centre is very beneficial both on and off the rock. Yoga and the eastern martial arts benefit from many centuries of refining this focus and it may feel familiar to climbers who also practise these disciplines.

Every joint in our body moves in curves, tracing arcs, ellipses and circles as we move. When you fancy a meditative experience, pick a pleasant route and allow yourself to flow up it in a series of interlinking arcs.

Exercise 17: The Butt Squeeze

This progression focuses on exploiting the biggest muscles of the body, the buttocks, for stability in static positions. Pull onto a vertical wall and arrange yourself on four holds, in a star shape with widely spread arms and legs:

> Without moving your trunk or hips, slowly take a hand off the wall, pause and place it again. Notice the changes in effort and tension in your body. Repeat this with the other hand and again with each foot in turn, being careful not to move your torso at all.

You have just tuned into some of the stability demands of climbing such as the extra effort involved each time a limb disengages from the wall and where in the body the forces are dealt with.

> Repeat the exercise above on the same four holds but this time squeeze your glutes (buttocks) tight each time you move a limb. Sense the difference it makes to your stability.

The loads on your body have not changed between these two exercises, you have simply shifted them to different muscle groups. Core engagement works to improve our climbing by moving effort from the most overworked muscles of the arms and shoulders to muscles working well within their capacity.

Climb an easy vertical route, squeezing the glutes for the duration of every hand move and only relaxing them when both hands are back on holds.

What effect did this have on your hip position?

How does it feel if you try to keep the glutes tense for foot moves?

What is it like on steeply overhanging terrain?

What is it like on thin slab climbs?

youtu.be/5vatkX_-KCg

Exercise 18: Hip and Hand Progression

> Combine the **Butt Squeeze** with the **Hip and Hand** drill: For the duration of every hand move, the glutes must be squeezed and the same hip must be against the wall as the moving hand.

Strong Vs Light

You will have noticed that to stabilise yourself for a hand move requires a certain level of glute effort, but not every move needs full tension. As with all muscular effort, there is a sliding scale where true efficiency comes from using *just enough effort* to achieve the task. You may also sense that tensing the glutes for more than a moment makes it tricky to employ momentum. Static hand moves are the easiest to perform when you are fixed in place by tension. Dance choreographer Rudolf Laban described the two ends of the spectrum as **Strong** versus **Light** positions. Any position on a climb can be held anywhere on this spectrum. Strong positions offer maximum stability and security on poor holds, whereas light positions allow maximum relaxation for recovery and economy. Boulderers typically master one end of the spectrum and trad climbers the other. Every type of climber would benefit from the ability to move fluidly back and forth on the spectrum according to the demands of each climb.

youtu.be/TepYEbZ7ass

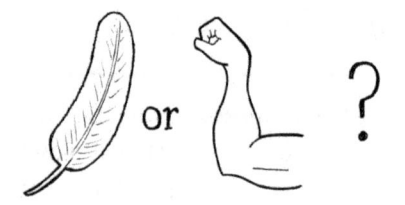

Be mindful of this as you explore more dynamic moves:

Using Momentum

All climbers tend to intuitively use their core, focused around their centre of mass, to generate momentum when needed. The next section is about exploiting that skill to its full potential.

Tensing the glutes can help reduce arm effort during static hand moves but we still need to work hard elsewhere to create that tension, particularly on steeper terrain. For the duration of every hand move, the other hand is holding doubly hard to keep us on the wall or rock. Momentum has the potential to significantly increase our efficiency here: using a dynamic movement to temporarily take weight off the holding hand bypasses some of this arm effort.

Dynamic Movement and Risk

Using momentum is sometimes perceived as an uncontrolled and high risk way of climbing. However, when performed skilfully, it improves efficiency of movement - try walking without it - and when used accurately can be performed consistently and safely. For a trad climber onsighting a bold route, momentum may be used very subtly for small hand flicks and foot bumps, while static reaches will be necessary for committing moves carrying serious risk. In contrast are redpoint or hard boulder attempts where every move can be performed as a deadpoint, allowing fast and economic passage through many hard sequences. Nearly every hand move can also be performed statically if you are strong enough. Only purposeful practice is going to give you the skills to use dynamic movement and avoid relying on strength.

Using the centre of mass to create momentum is the most effective way to move with minimal effort. Compare raising your centre of mass with momentum, as when jumping, to raising it by doing a pull up. How many jumps can you do versus number of pull-ups?

If we utilise those same leg muscles and techniques for our climbing wherever possible, we save our arms for when we really can't avoid pulling hard.

Momentous Moves – The Four Springs

In 2010 Scottish climber Dave MacLeod published his first book, *9 out of 10 Climbers Make the Same Mistakes*. It has since become a landmark book on holistic climbing improvement, introducing the climbing world to the different types of momentum move.

In this chapter I will build on MacLeod's foundation and explore further the place these moves have within general climbing movement. I have divided momentum-based hand moves into four distinct types:

- The Pendulum
- The Corkscrew
- The Leg Thrust
- The Core Pop

These moves and their variations will cover almost every hand move you will make!

These are detailed practical exercises with great potential for confusion and gnashing of teeth. For the greatest chance of success take this book and the accompanying videos with you when first trying them. Videoing yourself will help with gathering feedback. A vertical patch of bouldering wall covered in big holds is an ideal starting point.

Core

Exercise 19: The Pendulum

This is for a single hand move reaching to the side, when face-on to the wall. Position yourself face-on to the wall on four good holds, with hands at an equal height. Look left and choose a target handhold for your left hand that can be reached without moving either foot. Sink down onto bent legs, knees pointing outwards, until both arms are straight. This is the starting position.

Keeping your arms as straight as possible, use your legs to draw your hips back right, then swing your hips leftward, moving your left hand to the target hold as you do.

---

youtu.be/umxTDNi5qNo

Picture your centre of mass as a pendulum being drawn back right and then released so it can swing left to bring the hold within reach. All the initial effort comes from the legs, followed by a relaxed swing with just enough momentum to halt at the new handhold. Repeat this five times moving towards the left with the left hand, then towards the right with the right hand. Each time inspect your finish and start positions carefully. To prevent your body swinging back again, the core needs to engage in order to stabilise you at the new hold. If you feel like an orangutan, you're doing it right!

One of the aims of mastering The Four Springs is to ingrain the easiest, most efficient way to perform any given hand move. The infinite variables within climbing mean that this won't always be possible on the holds available on a given route. However, if the perfect version is well rehearsed, you have a good chance of spotting opportunities to get close to it in your everyday movement. Below is a list of criteria to strive for at the end of every hand move – use it to 'quality assure' your technique on The Four Springs:

The Ideal Finish Checklist

- Arms both straight, body low on the holds

- Supply and demand: momentum from the hips runs out just as your hand meets the target hold. This confirms you have exactly matched the amount of effort required to the demand of the move.

- Zero movement of the centre of mass after the target hold is caught

- Body drawn into the wall with glutes and core engaged

Troubleshooting

If both arms finish bent, you may be habitually straightening your legs. Check they are both bent to keep you as low as possible and avoid 'standing up' mid-move. Pulling with the arms to finish a move happens if you haven't created enough momentum - try a harder kick at the start of the move. Wobbling or pivoting after you've caught the hold suggests core tension is low - squeeze those glutes as you hit the target and remain motionless until you feel stable.

Exercise 20: The Corkscrew

This is for a single hand move upward when side-on to the wall, sometimes known as an Egyptian, or backstep move. It is the most complex of the four springs to perform so approach this exercise with plenty of energy and focus. Position yourself facing to the right, side-on with your left hip within six inches of the wall, on four good holds. Your hands should be level with each other, as should your feet. Look up and choose a target hold to move your left hand to that is directly overhead, or up and to the left of you. To avoid complicating things, ensure the target hold is reachable from your existing footholds so you don't end up standing on one leg. Sink down onto bent legs, knees pointing rightwards, until both arms are straight.

> Keeping the right arm straight, pivot your hips counter clockwise a little to face the wall, then spin them powerfully clockwise into the wall, extending your legs simultaneously to reach the target hold on a straight left arm.

During all of this your right arm can remain straight. The initial counter clockwise 'unwinding' hip motion is like the crouch before a standing jump – it's the run-up into the move for your centre of mass. The powerful twisting movement generated by your centre of mass brings the left shoulder high as you extend your legs to reach the target hold, creating a corkscrew path with your centre of mass. The corkscrew rotation should

youtu.be/1p0yTrIyOPw

continue all the way until your hips finish facing slightly outward – the belly button should be pointing away from the wall at about 45 degrees at the end of the move. Repeat this exercise several times on both left-hand moves (facing right) and on right-hand moves (facing left).

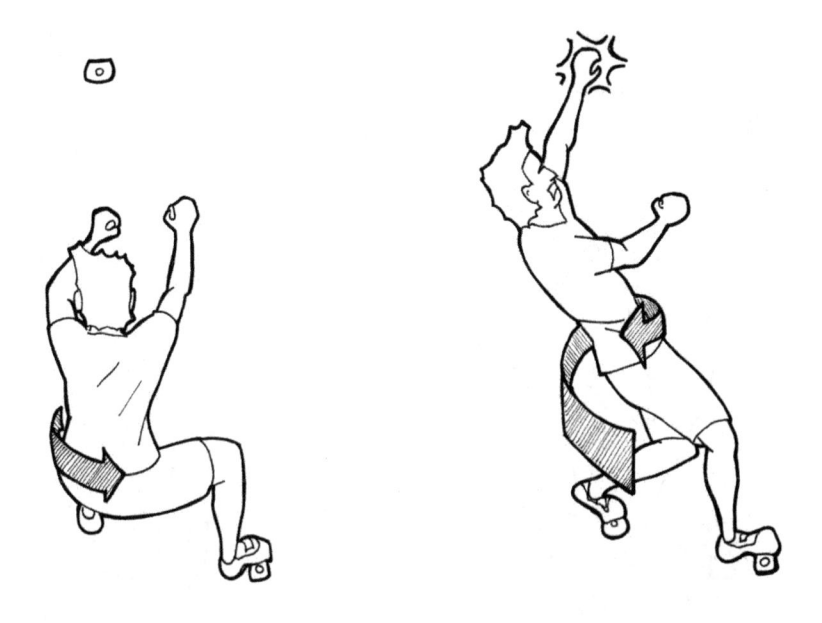

Now investigate the same move with a different focus:

Exercise 21: Knee-Throw Variation

Position yourself side-on, facing right as for The Corkscrew. Keeping the right arm straight, rotate your left knee back to the left (opening the hips) then throw it hard to the right and down. Allow your hips, trunk and shoulders to spin after it, extending up to the target hold as you rotate.

youtu.be/0zKeJY9iCbM

Monitor closely how every move feels and compare to the checklist below.

The Ideal Finish Checklist

- Arms both straight

- Supply and demand: momentum from the hips runs out just as your hand meets the target hold

- Zero movement of the hips after the target hold is caught

- Body drawn into the wall with glutes and core engaged

Troubleshooting

If you over extend either leg you will catch the target hold on a bent arm. Aim to 'only just' reach the target hold. If you don't corkscrew vigorously enough, you will run out of momentum and bend the lower arm to finish the move.

Once you get a feel for it, you may recognise The Corkscrew as a single-hand move from **Exercise 5: Hip and Hand** in Chapter One. The drill can be used to embed the corkscrew until, after many repetitions, you spiral lightly up the walls!

Exercise 22: The Leg Thrust

This is a single hand move upwards, facing the wall, often called a deadpoint move. It is also the first of the Four Springs that cannot generally be performed with two straight arms for the duration. Take a front-on position on the wall, again with feet level and hands level on good holds. Position the hands at about shoulder height when both legs are straight. Look up and pick a target hold for your left hand which is close to full reach directly above you. To begin, sink down from your start holds onto straight arms.

> Drop briefly down lower onto your legs and spring upward with a leg thrust. Your centre of mass should travel up in an arc curving first outward, then inwards to finish at the wall just as your left hand reaches the target hold on a straight arm.

Imagine you are a space rocket for this move: your legs are the thrusters propelling you into space and your right arm is the tail fin, guiding and steering but not providing power. Intimidating dynos often take this form but finish with two or more limbs off the wall. The principles remain the same regardless. To maximise success you need to focus on the legs and footholds for initial power, while your centre of mass traces a curve that is either moving towards the wall or motionless at the point at which you catch the finish hold.

Practice leg thrusts with either hand, on a variety of different-sized holds and for varying lengths of moves. Try these variations to help focus on engaging the core at the deadpoint of the move:

youtu.be/bbTyBqMZ-jE

Core

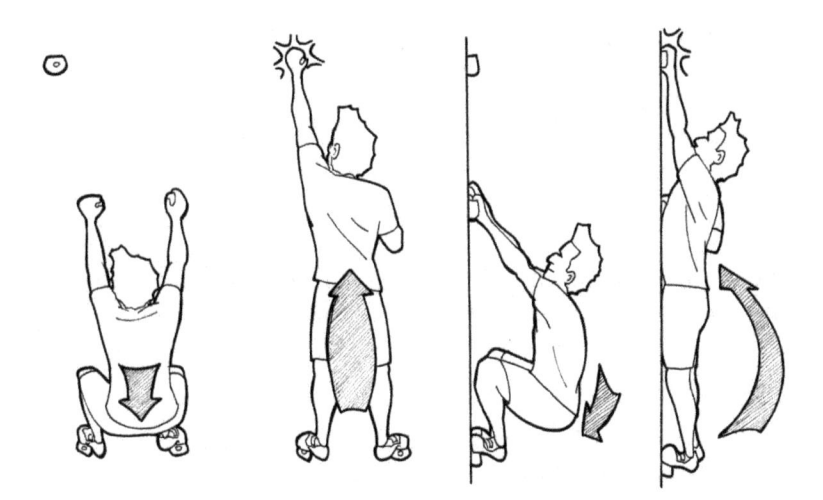

Glue Bellybutton

> Repeat the Leg Thrust but this time focus on super-gluing your bellybutton to the wall as you catch the target hold. Aim for zero hip movement after you've caught it.

Notice how the **Butt Squeeze** contributes to this exercise. Compare the shoulder effort involved if you keep a soft core while doing it. Try it on a wall overhanging by 20 degrees or more and observe the change in load on your core.

Exercise 23: One-Hand Variation

Repeat the Leg Thrust but let go with the lower hand just before you catch the target hold.

Performed on small holds or pockets, this is a stern test of hand accuracy, core control and mastery of dynamic movement. Sense the additional increase in core load and the great demand for timing and accuracy in the movement.

The Ideal Finish Checklist is the same as in Exercise 21, but only one hand is on a target hold and the arm should be straight.

Troubleshooting

With too much momentum or leg extension, you will either catch the hold on a bent arm or drop onto it, causing unnecessary finger stress. Too little and you'll lock, pull and reach with the assisting arm. If your feet pop off, your core needs to be engaged more at the end of the move. If you pivot or lurch sideways after catching the hold, you may have picked a slightly offset hand move and could try this:

Hold the finish position in the way that feels most natural and take a mental snapshot of where your centre of mass is in space. Now return to the start of the move and trace a curve with your centre of mass that goes directly to the finish position you just noted.

youtu.be/2o1KRrzkg2k

Often the climber catches a hold but then fails trying to control the swing or pivot afterwards, something which can be avoided by moving straight to the end position.

If you hit the hold but your hips are moving outward, downward or sideways at the time, you will fall in that direction unless it's a mega jug.

Exercise 24: The Core Pop

Have you ever stared at the next hold, seen it's within reach but known that if you let go to move a hand, you will fall? This is the time to unleash an emergency Core Pop or one of its variations.

This is a single hand move in a front-on position, from straight legs and either bent or straight arms. A Core Pop works for short 'within reach' hand moves when holds are not positive enough to Leg Thrust from. Establish yourself in a face-on position to the wall or rock, with good feet and straight legs but poor hands and bent arms. Pick a target handhold that is within reach. This is your start position.

> Draw your hips and torso out from the wall and spring them quickly back towards it, moving a hand to the target hold as you do so.

As you try moving each hand to different holds, sense how much of the thrust comes from pulling with the arms and how much comes from the core and back. If you find it hard not to pull, try picturing a wave of force starting at your toes, rolling up your body and throwing you towards the rock as it travels.

As the path of your centre of mass is short in comparison to the previous three moves, you have less time to make a move before momentum runs out. Short snatches, readjustments and moving the same hand twice in

youtu.be/0kQnXAgcfrs

a row all suit this approach. Locking off really hard and reaching strenuously is the static alternative but this is not great if the holds are poor.

Depending upon your contact points, there is a range of increasingly tenuous variations that all involve thrusting bodyweight inward, briefly allowing a limb to move.

Exercise 25: Shoulder Pop Variation

> Position yourself for a Core Pop, but with legs as wide apart as possible and straight. Keeping your hips glued to the wall, draw back your shoulders and head and throw them inward as you move a hand.

You will notice that the weight of your head and shoulders buys less time to move than throwing your centre of mass does. When very wide footholds, high core tension or opposing heel hooks prevent hip movement, a Shoulder Pop is often the next best option.

youtu.be/WY9aD9zLnBI

Core

Exercise 26: Hip Pop Variation

Position yourself for a Core Pop but with hands fully spanned out to either side. Keeping your head and chest against the wall, draw out your hips and pop them in as you make a short fast hand move.

These are useful when arms are at full stretch or pressing outward, or face and shoulders are pinned to the wall. Any movement of the legs will assist with generating spring from the hips. Foot swaps can also be performed efficiently with a Hip Pop or Core Pop – pick a tiny foothold and try it out.

youtu.be/JjQRLmUvg-A

Core

Exercise 27: Head Fling Variation

Position yourself for a Core Pop, but with the widest, poorest feet and hands you can manage - think starfish. Choose a nearby hold to move to, or plan to bump your hand up an arête or edge. Keeping your body stuck to the wall, tilt your head right back on your neck and fling it forward – carefully - snatching to the new hold as you do.

The 'Glasgow Kiss' of rock climbing, these look and feel pretty ridiculous to the uninitiated. However as an all-out short move, they can prove very useful. Watch any really hard climbing footage and you will see Head Flings deployed for very short hand moves such as slapping up arêtes. Our heads weigh about one stone so it's not going to buy lots of time, but try repeating the same moves statically and you will soon feel the difference.

youtu.be/3OMYp5MCRs4

Core

Geeks' Corner

Further Obscure Variants

While developing new boulder problems on some very abrasive granite, I locked horns with a lip traverse that had a finger-shredding combination of quartz crystal studded slopers for hands and almost useless vertical smears for feet. After three sessions, numerous bleeding finger tips, tape, sandpaper and super glue, I discovered an exaggerated chicken-peck allowed me to hold the crux! With my 'forward head-thrust' refined, the problem finally yielded on the next session and became 'Haptic Martyr'.

The moral of the story? Creativity is king in climbing. There are no constraints on how you can create momentum. Here are some more esoteric variants of the Four Springs:

- **Shoulder Roll** – A vigorous spin of the torso, initiated by throwing one shoulder past the other for big cross-overs and reach-throughs

- **Arm Fling** - Creating extra upward force by flinging an arm in the direction you want to travel

- **Leg Fling (a.k.a Pogo, Ninja Kick)** - Kick that leg for some upward and sidewards momentum.

Play with these, and then invent a few of your own.

The supply and demand principle - matching the supply of momentum to the demand of the move - can be explored in greater depth. Experiment with these five variables next time you are stopped by a move:

1. Move speed
2. Size

3. Load on individual limbs and overall load on the core
4. Hold quality
5. Metabolic demand – could the power used compromise the rest of the climb?

The centre of mass plays a leading role in this chapter and further investigation of it is encouraged. Many Eastern movement disciplines such as yoga, tai chi and aikido explore the principle of body centre in great depth.

If you're after more of the theory that underpins movement centres, balance and general climbing technique, Dan Hague and Douglas Hunter's ground-breaking text *The Self-Coached Climber* gives a solid practical introduction to the background physics.

Postural habits and functional movement strongly influence how climbers move on the rock. *Stability, Sport and Performance Movement* by Joanne Elphinston is a good springboard into the subject.

Rock Climbing Technique

notes

Chapter 4

Tension

'*I feel like I've been hacked*'

So said Jen after trying some of the following exercises for the first time. She had made a startling personal discovery: the muscle tension she previously associated with feelings of unstoppable rising anxiety could simply be switched off at will.

Muscular tension dictates the smoothness and ease of our movement. Too little and we wilt onto the handholds or sag loosely on overhangs. Too much and we claw our way jerkily upward with breath held, elbows out and calves jiggling. Muscle tension is inextricably linked to our mental state and we can control it both consciously and unconsciously. Feeling tense isn't generally regarded as a positive state and psychological battles usually underpin unwelcome muscle tension. Over time, unconscious stress-related tension can become a habitual part of our movement, even long after we believe we are generally comfortable climbing. This unnecessary tightness is the focus of this chapter. We will explore muscle tension and seek to improve performance through a better understanding of our situation.

The Maximal Relaxed Effort Paradox

Don't underestimate just how hard it is to combine maximal effort and relaxation on a climb. This is probably the toughest skill to acquire in this book, and the hallmark of a true master of any movement discipline, be it climbing, athletics or dance. Relaxing whilst trying really hard is a top tier skill, taking years of deliberate attention to master. For every great climber that glides effortlessly up hard terrain, there are a dozen super-strong ones that gasp, squeeze, slap and grimace on the same ground. Often they are physically stronger than the better performer – imagine how hard they could climb if they mastered relaxed movement!

Hello Muscles

For this awareness exercise we will use your internal measuring scale to gauge muscle tightness. The scale runs from ten - as tight as possible, down to zero – as relaxed and lengthened as possible. Pick a lead route well within your grade. The exercise is described in a leading context but it can also be done top-roping or on a bouldering wall, pausing every five hand moves.

Exercise 28: The Tension Tester

As you are about to pick up the rope to clip it into the first quickdraw, pause. Tense both calf muscles right up to ten and hold for five seconds – this will be painful – then relax them down to zero, sinking deeply into your heels. Now pick up the rope and make the clip. Repeat this at every clip as you ascend.

Notice your anxiety level - does it vary according to how tight your calves are?

On your tension scale, what do your calves normally score on a climb?

Does the score change as you get further above your last runner, higher up the route or more pumped?

Repeat the Tension Tester focusing on the following muscle groups, each time pausing to conduct the test before making each clip.

- Shoulders – pull them forward and up to your ears as you tense them

- Hands and elbows – grip really hard

- Jaw and neck

- Belly

Strive for control, trying to isolate just that muscle group and checking to see if other areas are tightening too. Perhaps you can now identify where you habitually hold muscle tension during 'times of excitement'. Understanding how it feels when our muscles are both very tense and very relaxed can give us handy reference points, allowing us to proactively adjust mid-climb.

Muscle tension is linked to increased anxiety levels as part of our primal fight-or-flight response to perceived threats. Tense muscles are very useful for fighting a sabre-toothed tiger or quickly running away. While this is a good survival skill, sometimes tension is inadvertently coupled with factors other than danger. An off-piste skier should rightly be nervous when stood in deep, unstable snowpack, but what if they were on a flat ground with no chance of avalanche? In the same way, some climbers feel more stressed and tense as they become more pumped. If they are one inch above a padded floor, this is unhelpful. De-coupling tension from pump, proximity to quickdraws, height above the ground or exposure can be very effective. There is plenty of danger in climbing where sound judgement and genuine anxiety should be directed.

Hello Breathing

'Movement rides on the flow of breath'

– choreographer and physical therapist Irmgard Bartenieff

Breathing, like muscle tension, can be controlled both by conscious effort and our unconscious mind. Some say it's a magical gateway between the two realms. Whatever you believe, awareness and breath control is undoubtedly a powerful tool for managing tension and anxiety. As anxiety rises we shift from slow deep belly breaths to fast shallow chest breaths. Deliberate relaxed breathing can assist in reducing unnecessary tension and anxiety. Try the following exercises on easy top roping or bouldering terrain:

Exercise 29: The Breath Sink

> Pause after three hand moves. Take a steady, deep breath in through the nose, feeling your waist expand in all directions as your diaphragm fills. Slowly blow all your tension out, allowing yourself to sink softly onto the holds. Repeat this every three moves as you ascend.

Can you maintain a tall engaged posture, lengthening the spine as you sink?

Is your breath filling your belly area, rather than lifting the chest and shoulders?

Can you focus on a slow out-breath that takes longer than inhaling?

Now try it on an easy lead:

> When you are about to pick up the rope to clip the first quickdraw, pause and repeat the process above, blowing all your tension out and sinking onto the holds before picking up the rope and making the clip. Repeat this at every clip as you ascend.

Notice how your tension differs when leading.

Choose a muscle group where you felt particular tension in the Tension Tester exercise and this time synchronise relaxing only those muscles with the Breath Sink practised above:

Exercise 30: Sink to Zero Progression

> Repeat the steps above but this time when you blow your tension out, sink your chosen muscles to zero. Repeat before every clip.

Breathing for Power and Stability

Once the moves start getting harder, breath also plays a role in providing stability. Compare the strength and rigidity of an unopened fizzy drink can to an empty one. Our torso responds in a similar way when filled with pressurised air. A friend of mine once experimented with this by repeatedly jumping out of a tree. He stopped after kneeing himself hard in the chin. We'll take a less committing approach:

Exercise 31: Core Pressure

Create a hard single hand move that stretches you out on the wall. Perform it with full lungs, then empty lungs and compare the two. Repeat it starting with full lungs, exhaling as you move. Finally repeat it beginning empty, inhaling as you move.

Observe the difference in stability of the start and finish positions, and how powerful or feeble you felt when initiating the move. An inflated diaphragm provides maximum trunk stability, which is what you need if faced with a very difficult start or finish position. A controlled exhale may assist with power depending on the move. These techniques are all a compromise with your body's oxygen requirements. Make it a habit to resume deep belly breathing for oxygen and tension management wherever possible.

Move Like It's Easy

Effortless performance is a hallmark of mastery in any sport. If this is what you aspire to, it needs to be rehearsed. When you are regularly trying really hard, it is easy to ingrain a 'high effort' style. Grimacing, gasping and over-gripping are best saved for just a few moves, while treating everything else as if it's easy for you, regardless of the truth.

Exercise 32: Slackjaw

Pick a steeply overhanging route that will exhaust you in fewer than thirty hand moves. Ascend with a relaxed, calm expression and a slack jaw. Focus on maintaining this expression regardless of your fatigue levels.

Tension in the jaw from the 'power gurn' inhibits head, neck and shoulder movement, in turn making fluid and dynamic movement harder. Remember that no-one can see your face as you climb so you might just get away with that gormless expression.

Geeks' Corner

'Parasitic Tension' is the term given by Todd Hargrove in his excellent book *Better Movement*. It captures the rather insidious nature of long term muscle tension that hides below our conscious awareness. Far greater strength is required to climb well with excess tension, so it's well worth exploring further.

Progressive Muscle Relaxation (PMR) is the technique used in the Tension Tester exercise, an established psychology technique that merits further investigation for the curious.

The Slackjaw is designed to counter Facial Fixing. This is the term coined by Joanne Elphinston to describe the overbite, tongue-out or grimace that can appear on our hardest moves. It is a sign of a stability and control issue and, whilst it may help you complete a move, it won't transfer well. It's a compensatory technique and mastering the move without it carries far more learning value.

The subjects of breath and tension serve as powerful tools for helping climbers to better understand anxiety on the rock. There is a vast amount of research within the broad field of psychology. I'd encourage exploring beyond the confines of sports psychology into social, behavioural and cognitive psychology.

Rock Climbing Technique

notes

Chapter 5

Move Reading

Fast, flowing and decisive movement needs confidence in your choice of moves. This confidence is developed by time spent making deliberate movement decisions and reviewing how successful they were. Hesitant climbing, dithering on cruxes or staring at foothold options for more than a second or two can all stem from move reading inefficiencies.

Move reading is about accurately anticipating every opportunity to apply your skill in the most efficient fashion. In most climbers this process is left to chance. For many, their intuitive approach masks a host of inefficiencies of which they are unaware. A high level of bodily awareness is fundamental to skilful move reading. Be prepared to wrestle mentally in order to become more efficient in this area.

The next three exercises are best done on boulder problems, ideally with a partner. A tablet or smart phone on which to video them can be useful too.

Hello Memory: Move Recall

First let's explore your ability to recall your movement on rock.

Pick an easy boulder problem that is unfamiliar to you. Climb it once and when you have finished, try and recall the exact hand and foot sequence you used, in the correct order.

Which was easier to recall, the hand or foot moves?

Which bits stood out – the start, finish, or hardest part?

To double check your accuracy, climb it again until you are sure of every move. This may take time and perseverance!

If you are anything like me, your lazy mind will have been tempted to complete this exercise by other means. There are many ways to bypass the skill of move recall. Watching and copying other climbers, gathering beta and looking up videos of your objectives are just a few. They may help you complete that particular climb quicker, but at the expense of learning. Those who consistently flash and onsight close to their physical limit have put the hard yards in, working things out on their own. If you are outside the average height demographic, or climb alone, you will be forced to confront this much earlier in your career. It has enormous value and allows you full ownership of your successes, which is great for motivation.

Exercise 33: Plan, Climb, Review

Now test your forecasting skills on an easy boulder problem that you haven't climbed before:

> Without touching the problem, predict every move you will make in as much detail as possible. Your partner needs to remember these predictions.
>
> Now disregard your plan and climb it in whichever way seems easiest.
>
> Finally, review how you climbed it in comparison to your original plan.

This is where good move recall, a watchful partner or a video can come in handy. Remember that excellent recall is the skill to aim for so that eventually you can repeat this exercise alone with ease.

What were the differences between the plan and execution?

Was your height, reach and flexibility as you anticipated?

Which was more accurate – your predicted hand or foot sequence?

You will hopefully have gathered lots of information about what you anticipated, what you did and how the climb really feels.

> Refine your sequence over repeated ascents. Continue until you believe you have found the most effortless way in which to climb the problem and you can recall it exactly.

During this exercise you can apply any appropriate technical skills that you have explored in the book. For example, can you climb it with **Seriously Silent Ninja Feet** or **Two Feet On** or using the **Four Springs**?

These are some of the measures I use to judge the success of an ascent. Develop your own and benchmark against them as you refine problems.

Reflective practice is the process we are using here to sharpen our skills. When you are feeling energised to learn, try an easy boulder circuit of up to twenty problems applying this to every one: **Plan** a sequence before you pull on, **Climb** the problem, **Review** your sequence. If you think you could climb it better, plan how you will do this and repeat the ascent. Otherwise move onto the next problem. This is a mentally demanding session, not to be done after a tough day at work.

Over time, with purposeful practice, the gap between your predicted plan and the most efficient method will narrow. As it does, you will find yourself flashing and onsighting harder moves and positioning hands and feet more quickly. Redpointing and projecting will become more streamlined, involving less attempts and minimal time repeating mistakes.

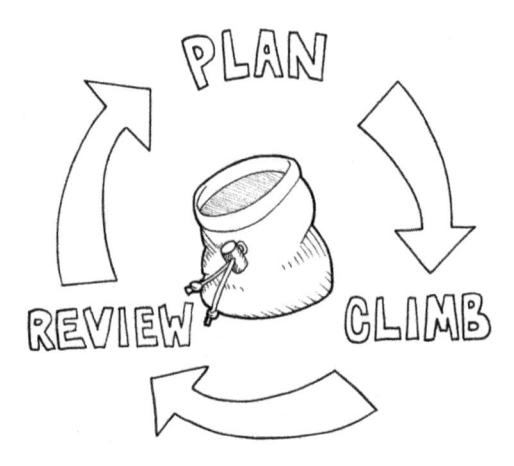

From Boulders to Routes

Delaying move reading until you have started a route means you will have lots to think about while climbing and, as a result, climb slowly. This additional time on the climb will tax your arms and could instead be spent on harder routes, if only you could read more moves in advance.

While a significant amount of information only becomes available in the midst of an onsight battle, doing everything we can to ensure this is minimised will buy us the time and mental space to juggle the other demands on our attention. While redpointing and bouldering, there's no good reason not to have everything from foot moves to breathing pre-planned if it allows faster, more relaxed movement and success in fewer attempts.

Here are two approaches to refine move reading in onsight climbing:

Exercise 34: Chunking

Many subtle details of a route only reveal themselves as you get near to them. Between the more complex and blind sections of climbs are usually sections that are easier to read and predict. Sometimes these are just rest positions, a foot ledge or a well-chalked jug. Pick a lead route at your '95 percent onsight chance' level, and on rock rather than resin if that's where your goals lie.

Visually split the pitch into several chunks, or sections. The breaks could be where there is a change in angle or difficulty, or perhaps a rest or gear placement opportunity. At these points on the route you will plan to inspect the next chunk in detail and plan your strategy for moving to the next break.

We are splitting a long pitch in to a series of boulder problems, allowing for the detailed planning to take place en-route at the best resting positions. Redpoint sport climbers may notice this tends to develop naturally as a tactic when projecting routes.

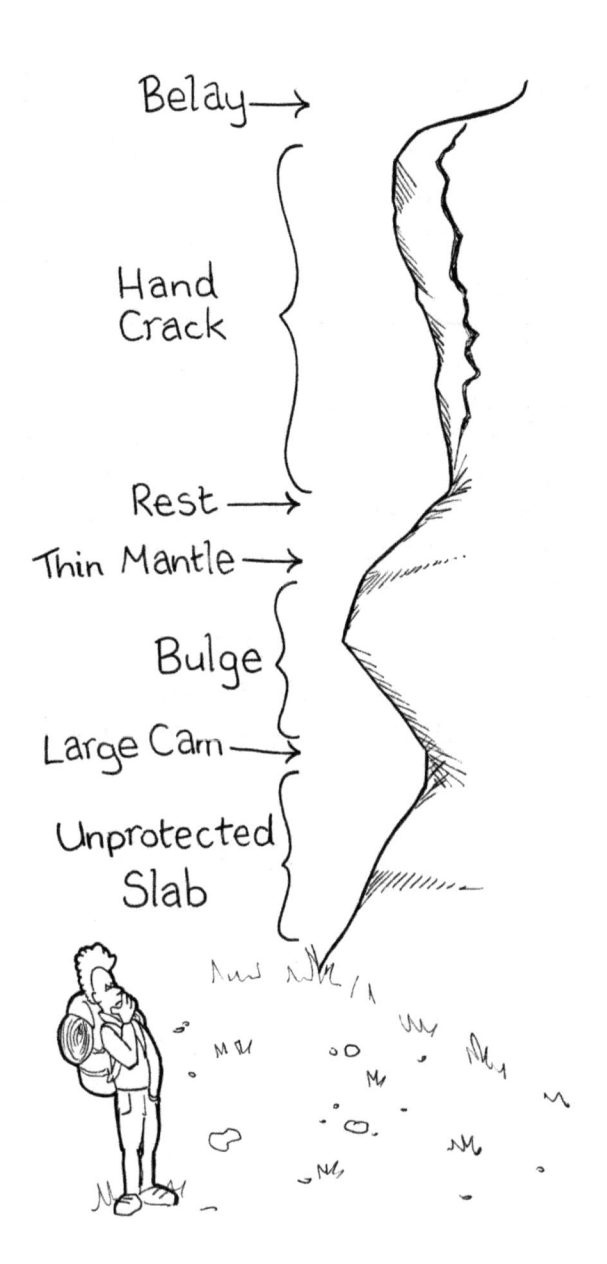

Exercise 35: Highlights

For uniformly angled wall climbs, indoor routes and 'sprint to the top' style routes this approach can complement the chunking approach. As for Chunking, choose a lead route at around your '95 percent onsight chance' level:

> Take no more than thirty seconds to read the hand sequence and then describe up to half a dozen highlights of the route to your belayer. These are the things you predict are most important to remember when climbing it. These may be crucial sequences, holds that are easy to miss, shake-out opportunities, decision points or similar.

Review your success with your belayer afterwards. How accurate were you? Is there anything you missed? Were any of the highlights irrelevant?

Move Reading

Pace and Rhythm

Decision making ability limits the pace of climbing for most novices. Sometimes habit means that pace remains unchanged even years after the climber has become much quicker at making movement decisions. Duration of effort has a direct impact on physiology – the slower you climb, the fitter you need to be. However, above a certain pace, precision starts to suffer and we either fall or overcompensate by pulling harder than necessary.

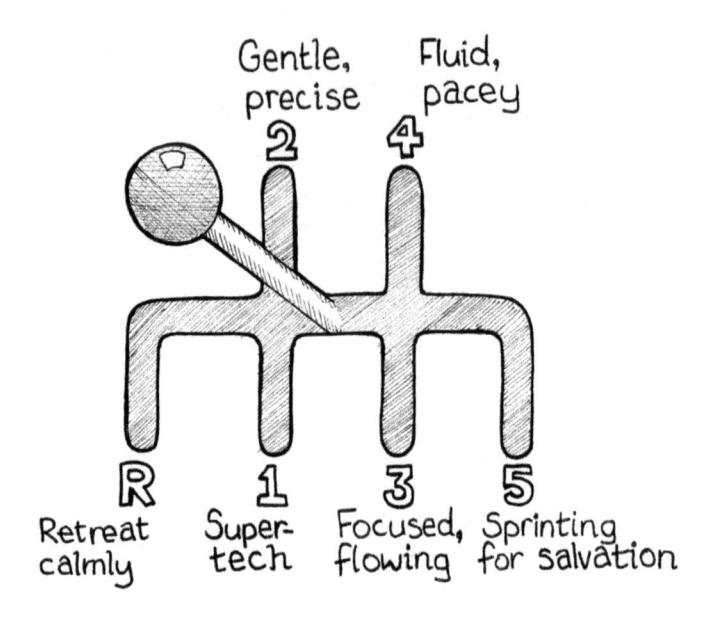

Gearbox diagram:
- R — Retreat calmly
- 1 — Super-tech
- 2 — Gentle, precise
- 3 — Focused, flowing
- 4 — Fluid, pacey
- 5 — Sprinting for salvation

Treading the fine line between 'slow crimpy static' and 'sketchy fast' requires the ability to change rhythm to suit the demands of each climb and every move within it. Experimenting with your default climbing speed is the key. How many gears are in your gearbox? Mastering accurate dynamic movement and excellent move reading will open the door to faster climbing with practice.

Exercise 36: Speed Chunking

Pick a route and, using the **Chunking** exercise, split it up into sections between rest points. Aim to climb each chunk as fast as possible *without* compromising on movement quality. This will vary according to what type of movement is within each chunk. Remember to make an accurate reading of the next chunk before you start up it.

If you redpoint or boulder, apply this to your projects and observe the effect it has on fatigue at different points.

The Gold Standard

When a skilled move reader looks at a climb, they visualise themselves climbing it. Some from a first-person view within themselves, and some from a third person view as if watching themselves on a screen. From this they anticipate not only the hand and foot sequence, but the body positions, the twisting and springing and the physical feel of the entire climb. Aspire to this standard when you are practising.

Taking it Outside

Transferring move reading ability from indoor routes to real rock is like moving from crayon sketches to oil painting. It's a big step to a more subtle and complex skill which takes years to truly master. Every downward glance presents numerous options for where to place each foot. Depending on the texture, friction and rock type, these skills will vary enormously and be led by principles of balance, rather than a simple choice of two or three coloured resin holds. If you have an opportunity to influence route setting indoors or have your own wall, setting with many tiny footholds will fast-forward your outdoor foot-move reading skills.

Geeks' Corner

Both the Chunking and Highlights exercises simplify a larger, more complex task for the climber.

If you really want to excel, learning every move on a route is the way to go. Excellent move prediction and recall become tools that can also aid with psychological factors. Visualisation techniques are a powerful way to increase the rate of learning and bring greater success on your hardest boulders and redpoints. Detailed mental rehearsal hinges on accurate recall of the moves. Explore visualisation within sports psychology if you would like to further exploit move reading skills.

Likewise, for trad onsights, high quality move reading can help manage anxiety levels by reducing the number of 'surprises' encountered on a pitch. If long runouts, big reaches and hidden holds can be anticipated, they are mentally easier to cope with. Chunking can also help reduce nerves as it helps to mindfully focus on the immediate challenge of the next few metres.

Move Reading

notes

Chapter 6

Strategy

'It's not how much you practise, it's how you practise'

— Swedish psychologist Anders Ericsson

LANGUAGE and experience are very different things. Reading this book without doing the exercises will leave your mind filled with a collection of abstract concepts. Pulling on to the rock or climbing wall and exploring through movement is where the learning journey really begins.

How you practice what you've learned will decide its potential to help you. Strategy in this context is about structuring your approach to improvement. If move reading is micro-tactics, this is mega-tactics, month by month, year by year. Formulate an effective strategy and you will see decades of improvement.

Focusing Your Play

Traditionally, keen climbers who add some structure to their physical training see better gains than those who just climb. The same approach can be applied to improving skilfulness. Adding structure increases learning speed and helps develop excellent movement - it is fundamentally about breaking and forming habits.

Whenever you climb, you are practising movement, be it good or bad and whether you choose to or not. The movements you perform most become your habits or style. They require very little mental effort, meaning you can remain relaxed and give your attention to other tasks whilst performing them.

Conversely, the moves you rarely perform become your 'anti-style', requiring a large amount of conscious attention to pull off.

Unfortunately, rock climbs don't care for style - the greatest climber is the one who can 'be like water' and morph their style as required by the route.

> *'Do not be assertive, but adjust to the object and you shall find a way around or through it. If nothing within you stays rigid, outward things will disclose themselves. Empty your mind, be formless. Shapeless, like water'*
>
> *- Bruce Lee*

Stress, be it fear of falling, failure or the unrelenting pump, demands a lot of mental attention. If you are stressed on a climb, your brain automatically opts for your most habitual movement because it requires less attention.

With the help of the exercises in this book you will become aware of a few of these habits, helpful or otherwise. The aim of structured practice is to train your weaknesses, neglect your habitual movements and fast-forward reinforcement of the least familiar techniques. This approach will give the broadest skill-set, allowing you to adapt to any terrain and style.

Purposeful Practice

Once you feel confident that you are able to observe your movement in any given exercise accurately, it is time to begin embedding the techniques deep in your unconscious and turning them into habits.

What does really good practice look like? It is practice that gives the optimum levels of retention (how it sticks in your mind) and transferability (how it can be adapted to all scenarios) at the fastest rate.

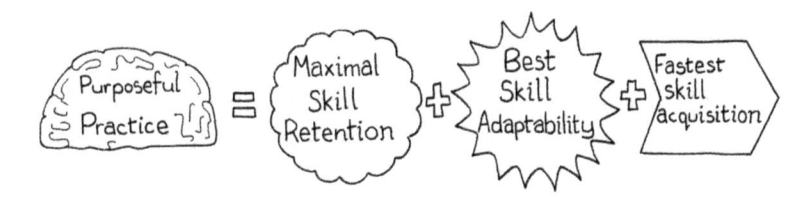

Purposeful Practice = Maximal Skill Retention + Best Skill Adaptability + Fastest skill acquisition

If you simply go climbing, the new skills you learn will only occur randomly. The exercises in this book are designed to repeatedly target a skill, thus taking the 'chance factor' out of your practice. Pick a skill you want to improve and repeat the exercise until it feels fluid and effortless. Apply it whilst leading on easy terrain and then on overhanging ground, graded routes and problems, differing rock types and in a broad variety of situations. Whilst training technique your agenda is simply to improve your movement. This means grades, style of ascent and 'getting to the top' are irrelevant – save them for when you are performing, and know the difference.

Stress Proofing

Gradually increase stress levels - forearm pump and psyche - during the drill to help embed the skill. This can be done by:

- Transferring from top-roping to leading

- Getting *really* pumped, then rehearsing the exercise

- Practising in front of lots of people

- Demonstrating to another curious climber

- Practising on routes or wall angles that intimidate you

- Using the skills in a competition

- Combining several of the above

Only consider a skill a useful one once you notice inefficient habits resurfacing whilst battling hard at performance levels on your chosen terrain - be that indoors or outdoors, on boulders, sport or trad routes. Aim to keep the 'technique scanner' on all the time, and return to easier climbing for deliberate practice of movement. This applies to every exercise in this book and is not a quick fix - think months and years.

Quality Standards: An Alternative Measure of Success

'We are what we repeatedly do. Excellence then, is not an act, but a habit'

- Aristotle

When you are climbing normally, what can you do to ensure you are always ingraining good movement habits? Set yourself some standards of movement quality that you'd like to reach to consider a climb successful.

Take pride in climbing a route in good style and have a mental checklist of criteria to quantify this. If I top out but don't meet my own measures, I'll be coming back to do better. Here are some examples from my own bouldering sessions:

Strategy

- Foot Placement: First time. Pause and repeat if bounced or adjusted.

- Hand placement: First time. Stop and repeat move if adjusted.

- Foot movement: Spring-Relax-Stick

- Hand movement: Core-Relax-Catch

Create a list of your own movement aims and be honest about when you want to meet them, and when it matters more that you top out cleanly!

Alongside movement standards are holistic approaches to aspire to. These are visulisation tools to help you construct a clear picture of how you aim to climb from start to finish on a route or problem. Experiment with the following tools and develop your own that capture your personal movement aspirations:

- The 'whole problem' approach: relaxed attack, one continuous movement

- Crisp, economical execution of every move

- Mindful movement - moving meditation

- The Glide - finding flow through movement

Think about how you aspire to climb and how you would like climbing to feel. Striving to replicate this in your practice hugely increases the chance of it happening regularly.

Building This Into Your Routine

The volume of purposeful practice you do will be directly linked to your rate of improvement – the more the better. Every time an elite athlete practises, it is solely for the purpose of getting better. This sort of focus could potentially make you an unsociable climber if you cannot find others equally focused, but with a little thought you can improve your climbing without dropping off the social radar.

A Balanced Approach: Traffic Light Sessions

Unless you are the ultra-psyched athlete mentioned above, then constant drilling of skills may gradually erode your motivation to climb. Managing your psyche against the optimum training program is fundamental. Many climbers give up on training programs because they don't find this balance.

Split your climbing into three types of session and choose which to undertake according to your motivation level on the day:

Green: *Super-psyched day*: You have lots of mental energy and are willing to focus intently on improvement. Aim for high-quality practice above all else. Work very hard on all your weaknesses, expect to fail lots and finish mentally fatigued.

Amber: *Fairly psyched*: You are keen but maybe a little tired. Aim for a mix of high-quality skills practice and fun, sociable climbing. Consolidate your existing skills with friends.

Red: *Mentally exhausted*: You want to climb to get a break from the rest of your life. Aim for gentle consolidation of existing skills and a high success rate, all on terrain you enjoy and feel relaxed upon. Eat nice snacks, drink tea and chat to everyone.

Sometimes you will arrive at the wall or rock feeling like it's a red-session day, but after half an hour get excited and shift gear towards amber or green. The trick is to set realistic expectations of your will power and recognise that many other things can drain it outside of climbing.

Tough physical training can fit into any of these sessions but it is more about mental energy levels. Even when you are mentally drained, pre-planned circuits or fingerboard training can still be completed.

Focusing on the Process

"The man who would polish his techniques must first polish his mind"

– 10th *Dan aikidoko Koichi Tohei*

Micro goal setting within a session can be a powerful tool to keep your attention on the learning that underpins a successful ascent. *Process goals* are those which require extra learning and increase your understanding of the process involved in the climb. In contrast *outcome goals* are measures of results and success levels.

Exercise 37: Micro Goals

On your way to the venue, set yourself one outcome goal and three process goals for a climbing session

---

For example, when trying a redpoint project, your session goals could be:

Outcome goal: Link from the third bolt to the top.

Process goal 1: Figure out exactly what the flagging leg is doing on the crux.

Process goal 2: Visualise climbing the route perfectly three times between each attempt.

Process goal 3: Identify four places to take a deep, relaxed breath mid-route.

On the way home review your session, with respect to each of your four goals.

I sometimes notice success in my process goals that I would have otherwise overlooked while feeling bad about failing to achieve a desired outcome. What looks to an outsider like an entire session of failed attempts, may actually have involved lots of valuable learning. This learning takes you closer to success and builds the skills that will help you on future climbs.

Geeks' Corner

You may have observed that a strong focus on mastering the process of climbing is encouraged, beyond achieving results. It can be challenging to shift your attention from getting to the top or ticking a grade. For many climbers that is where their attention defaults to and it is a tough habit to break. Are you motivated by an intrinsic desire for mastery and enjoyment of the process, or towards an outcome that will bring social or external rewards? A bit of both perhaps? Exploring the motivation behind your climbing may shed some light on this – Self-Determination Theory is a good place to start. A shift in attitude is sometimes necessary to allow a change in focus to happen. Carol Dweck's work on Growth Mindset is another great exploration of the subject and all the far-reaching benefits of being process-focused in your approach to life.

Skill Acquisition

Practising in a way that optimises retention and transferability typically results in *slower* but *better* skill acquisition than traditional methods of practice.

It may feel counterintuitive, but structuring your practice so that it is varied, rather than following a linear pathway, is supported by some interesting theory. Explore nonlinear pedagogy in skill acquisition if you are curious – it's an approach well suited to the variable demands of rock climbing.

The master strategist won't confine their approach to improving technique alone. Many elements of climbing remain outside the scope of this book. They include psychological elements of the sport, physical training and managing the inherent risks of climbing. There are some excellent texts on all these subjects. Neglect any of these areas of your development and you will fail to optimise your climbing performance.

Rock Climbing Technique

With a solid strategy, you can steadily progress in all areas, within every session.

Strategy

notes

Chapter 7

Quick Wins

Common Movement Problems

The common cold, flu, asthma, warts. Doctors see lots of these on a regular basis. Similarly, I diagnose certain technique issues more frequently than others.

Below are the movement issues I see most often in each climbing discipline. These are a good place to start if you are feeling bewildered by the options. However, just like mother said, you are unique and special, and you may be an exception to the norm with different challenges to overcome. The only sure way to know you are training your weaknesses is to explore the whole book, or hire a good coach. But if you're short on time, here are some ways to hedge your bets.

Traditional Climbing

Up to E3/5.11

For many trad climbers, anxiety dictates quality of movement. Prolonged periods of tension and stress on lonely leads have reinforced a tense, strenuous and static approach. Allowing anxiety levels to be dependent on proximity to gear placements, or how pumped you are, will make life unnecessarily tough. If this sounds familiar, aim to master the five exercises in Chapter Four, and Chunking from Chapter Five. Be honest with yourself about your falling fears as time spent reducing them could be invaluable. Until you can calm the babbling demons in your head, improving your technique will be very tough.

Beyond E3/5.11

Above these grades, sport climbing and trad habits cross over a great deal – see below for further tips, and apply them to your trad performances.

Sport Climbing and Bouldering

Boulderers and sport climbers are often drawn to physical training early in their progression, sometimes at the expense of other skills. Begin technique work with the priorities below if you're unsure.

Up to 6c/5.11 and V3 boulders

Fantastic footwork is usually top priority at this point. Bury yourself in Chapter One and after a suitable apprenticeship of purposeful practice, emerge like a hatching butterfly to flutter up your nemesis projects.

Quick Wins

6c - 7b/5.11-12 routes, V3-V8 boulders

For those climbing routes up to this level, pump-induced anxiety and tactics often surface as areas for development. Chapters Four and Five hold the key to progression here. If you are regularly complimented for being strong, it's likely that Chapter One will also serve you well and ensure that you are not compensating for dodgy footwork with bulging muscles. For boulderers, it is often the tactics (Chapter Five) and hand skills (Chapter Two) which need attention if you don't fall into the 'really strong' bracket.

7c/5.13 routes, V9 boulders and beyond

I have seen many very fit climbers operating at this level with poor skills in one area. Going through each exercise and seeking critical feedback from peers will be essential to maintaining progression and reducing frustration. The most common underused skills are core and momentum – check in with the Butt Squeeze, Finding Centre and Four Springs exercises in Chapter 3.

> *"You must unlearn what you have learned"*
>
> *- Yoda*

Rock Climbing Technique

notes

Conclusion

"There is no satisfaction whatever at any time. There is only a queer divine dissatisfaction, a blessed unrest that keeps us marching and makes us more alive"

Martha Graham
– American dancer and choreographer

Go To It!

It is never too early – or late - in your climbing career to focus on movement. The bottom line is that it is about what is most efficient for you and your build, flexibility and body shape. Only blame your failures on fitness as a last resort, be creative and experimental in your movement and embrace the process of problem-solving tricky moves.

Most importantly strive for excellence, not perfection. There is no destination where you will achieve total mastery, only the 'divine dissatisfaction' of always spiralling up towards a disappearing point.

Consider Coaching

Climbing is fundamentally a sport that is learned by experience. Coaching climbers in person is where the greatest impact can be made.

If you'd like to explore anything in this book further, improve faster, or discover the many things I haven't included, get in touch to arrange some coaching. I'm available for individual and group sessions, coach education courses and workshops.

www.johnkettle.com

I'd Love to Hear From You

This book represents perhaps the 10 percent of what I've learned and feel confident communicating in writing, drawings and videos. I'm on a lifelong learning journey through climbing and my understanding of it is constantly evolving. Your feedback on this book, your ideas on movement and your criticisms of my ideas are most welcome. Perhaps they will appear in a future edition!

Glossary

Auto belay: A mechanical device attached at the top of an indoor climb, designed to take the place of a top-rope belayer. With a retracting cable or webbing to clip into, it automatically tightens as you climb, and lowers if you let go.

Backstep: Standing on the outside edge, or little toe, of the foot

Beta: Information given about a climb, often about crucial moves, rests or gear placements

Bouldering: Climbing unroped on boulders or short walls, above crash pads or matting

Centre of mass: The point at which the body is balanced in space, it is the focal point of gravity's pull on the body.

Crimp/half crimp grip: A handhold position where the finger joint angle at the second knuckle is less than 90 degrees, usually on a small flat or incut hold. In a half crimp they are bent at the second joint by 90-120 degrees.

Crux: The hardest section of a climb, usually a single hand move or two.

Deadpoint: A dynamic hand move, where the weight is thrown to reach a handhold, aiming catch it at the 'dead point' in the body's momentum. Unlike a static move, the climber will usually fall if the hold is missed.

Dragging grip: A handhold position where the finger joint angle at the second knuckle is more than 120 degrees, on a small flat or incut shaped handhold. Usually the little finger is too short to be involved in this position. Also known as open grip or sloper grip.

Dyno: Any dynamic move – those moves that use momentum and cannot be paused mid-move.

Egyptian: A side-on body position, with one hip against the wall, and both feet pointing to side the climber is facing.

Flagging: A move or body position in which the climber stands on one leg and uses the other as a counterbalance to assist in keeping weight over the supporting foot.

Glutes: The two distinct buttock muscles - Gluteus Maximus

Groove: A vertically orientated corner, usually climbed using bridging techniques for the hands and feet.

Inside edges: Using the edge of the ball of the foot, just inside the big toe to stand on footholds.

Jamming: Wedging body parts into cracks in the rock to secure yourself, rather than holding on using muscular effort.

Jug: A large and incut handhold, easily held.

Lead Climbing: Roped climbing where the climber trails a rope down from them to a belayer on the ground, clipping it through either fixed or hand placed protection as they ascend, in order to protect against a fall.

Lock off: Holding a static position with one arm fully bent (hand by the same shoulder or lower) while reaching with the other arm.

Mantle: A climbing move in which downward pressure is applied with the hands to a ledge, lifting the body high enough to get the feet on that same ledge (as if climbing onto a mantleshelf). Usually used when no handholds are available.

Glossary

Onsight: Lead climbing a route on the first attempt, without prior information beyond the guidebook description.

Open hand grip: A handhold position where the finger joint angle at the second knuckle is more than 120 degrees, often used on a very sloping hold, also known as a drag grip.

Overhang: A rock face that is steeper than vertical.

PIP joint: Proximal Interphalangeal Joint – the finger joint that is closest to the knuckles.

Pocket: A hole used as a hold, often only big enough to take one or two fingers

Proprioception: The sense of the relative position of one's own body and strength of effort being employed in movement.

Pump: The burning sensation and weakening usually felt in the forearms when fatigued by climbing.

Quads: The thigh muscles running down the front of the upper leg from hip to knee - quadriceps

Redpoint/projecting: Climbing a route/problem after practising it one or more times.

Rock over: A move where the climber begins with one high foot, and then 'rocks over' their weight onto it before standing up on the foot.

Slab: A rock face at an angle less than vertical to the ground.

Sloper: A smooth downward sloping hold, usually requiring careful use of friction for success.

Somatics: A field within bodywork and movement studies which emphasises internal physical perception and experience.

Sports Climbing: Roped climbing using pre-placed bolts in the rock as protection when leading.

Rock Climbing Technique

Top rope: Climbing with a rope running from the belayer through anchors fixed at the top of the climb. This ensures the rope can support the climber at any point while they climb.

Trad: Traditional roped climbing, where the lead climber places protection in the rock as they climb, without recourse to bolts or other pre-placed equipment.

Traverse: Sideways climbing over a horizontal distance.

About the Author

John Kettle is a passionate rock climber and professional coach based in the Lake District of Northern England. He has been climbing for over 20 years, including first ascents of traditional climbs, mixed winter routes and numerous boulder problems. He has coached climbers of all abilities for more than 15 years in traditional and sport climbing and bouldering, and continues to help individuals improve their performance and enjoyment of climbing in all its forms. He is involved in the delivery and development of UK coaching qualifications and regularly provides seminars, workshops and courses for climbing coaches.

www.johnkettle.com

Milton Keynes UK
Ingram Content Group UK Ltd.
UKHW020754051024
449151UK00012B/580